BUSY ANTS

by Kristin L. Nelson

Lerner Publications Company • Minneapolis

This book is available in two editions:
Library binding by Lerner Publications Company, a division of Lerner Publishing Group, Inc.
Soft cover by First Avenue Editions, an imprint of Lerner Publishing Group, Inc.
241 First Avenue North
Minneapolis, MN 55401 U.S.A.

Website address: www.lernerbooks.com

Words in *italic* type are explained in a glossary on page 30.

Library of Congress Cataloging-in-Publication Data

Nelson, Kristin L.
        Busy ants / by Kristin L. Nelson.
            p.   cm. — (Pull ahead books)
        Summary: Introduces the behavior, life cycle, and physical characteristics of ants and describes how ant colonies work.
        ISBN-13: 978-0-8225-3775-5 (lib. bdg. : alk. paper)
        ISBN-10: 0-8225-3775-3 (lib. bdg. : alk. paper)
        1. Ants—Juvenile literature. [1. Ants.] I. Title.
    II. Series.
    QL568.F7N46 2004
    595.79'6—dc22   2003020820

Manufactured in the United States of America
2 3 4 5 6 7 — JR — 12 11 10 09 08 07

These two *insects* are working together.

What kind of insects are they?

These busy insects are ants.

They are moving leaves to make a nest.

Ants work together to help build
their nests.

Their nests are their homes.

A group of ants living together
in a nest is called a *colony.*

Most colonies of ants build rooms and tunnels underground.

Some colonies build a mound of dirt called an anthill above their nest.

Every ant in a colony
has a job to do.

This ant is building a tunnel.

The queen ant is the most important ant in the colony.

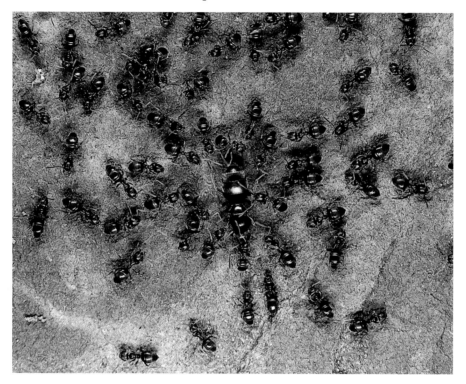

The queen ant's job is to lay eggs in the nest.

Worker ants build tunnels, find food, and protect the colony.

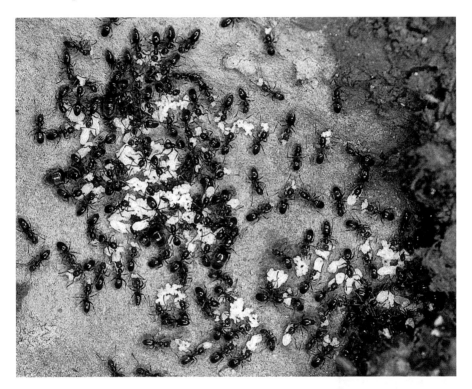

They also take care of the queen and her eggs.

Baby ants grow inside the eggs.
A *larva* hatches from each egg.

A larva looks like a small, fat worm.

Worker ants feed the larvas.
The larvas grow bigger.

Next, the larvas spin *cocoons.*
The larvas become *pupas.*

Which are the larvas here?
Which are the pupas?

A pupa does not eat.

It grows into an adult ant
inside its cocoon.

The new ant finally climbs out
of the cocoon.

Most new ants are workers.
They are ready to help the colony.

These ants are greeting each other by touching *antennas.*

Antennas stick out from an ant's head.

Antennas help ants to smell, taste, hear, and touch.

What body parts do you use to do these things?

Look! One of these ants is feeding the other.

What kinds of foods do ants eat?

Ants are *omnivores.*
They eat both plants and animals.

Ants eat seeds, worms, insects, and anything sweet.

An ant uses its strong jaws
to cut up food.

The jaws are called *mandibles.*
They move like scissors.

Ants also use their mandibles to carry food from one place to another.

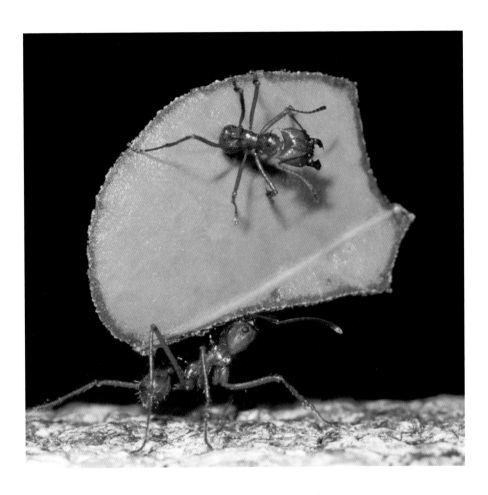

An ant can carry things that are much larger and heavier than it is.

These ants are carrying
parts of a leaf.

Ants have six legs.

At the end of each leg are two claws.

Claws help an ant to climb.

What else do ants use their claws for?

This ant is using its claws to hang upside down!

And these busy ants use their claws to carry a lizard egg to their nest. Ants make a great team!

KEY:

shows
where ants live

Find your state or province on this map.
Do ants live near you?

Parts of an Ant's Body

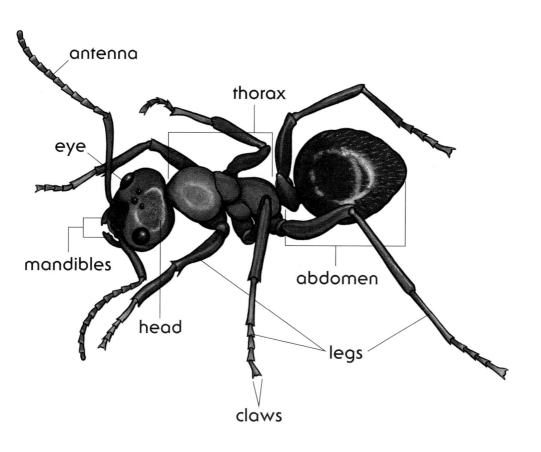

antenna

thorax

eye

mandibles

abdomen

head

legs

claws

Glossary

antennas: long, skinny feelers that stick out of an ant's head

cocoons: cases that cover pupas while they are changing into adult ants

colony: a group of ants that live together

insects: animals that have three main body parts and six legs

larva: the stage of an ant's life after it hatches from an egg

mandibles: jaws that ants use to hold, carry, and cut food

omnivores: animals that eat both plants and animals

pupas: young ants that are changing from larvas to adult ants

Hunt and Find

About the Author

Kristin L. Nelson loves writing books for children. Along with ants, she has written about several other animals for Lerner's Pull Ahead series. When she's not working on a book, Kristin enjoys reading, walking, and spending time with her husband and two children. She and her family live in Savage, Minnesota.

Photo Acknowledgments

The photographs in this book are reproduced with the permission of: © John Kohout/Root Resources, cover, p. 16; © Robert and Linda Mitchell, pp. 3, 4, 5, 6, 7, 8, 11, 13, 17, 18, 20, 23, 26, 31; © Bill Beatty/Visuals Unlimited, pp. 9, 15; © Larry Stepanowicz/Visuals Unlimited, p. 10; © Scott Camazine, pp. 12, 19; © Bill Glass/Root Resources, p. 14; © REMY AMANN-BIOS/Peter Arnold, Inc., p. 21; © Eric Soder/Photo Researchers, p. 22; © Louise K. Broman/Root Resources, p. 24; © Mark Moffett/Minden Pictures, pp. 25, 27.